Ocean, Tidal, and Wave Energy

Lynn Peppas

Crabtree Publishing Company
www.crabtreebooks.com

Crabtree Publishing Company

www.crabtreebooks.com

Author: Lynn Peppas
Editor: Susan Labella
Coordinating editor: Chester Fisher
Proofreaders: Molly Aloian, Crystal Sikkens
Project editor: Robert Walker
Production coordinator: Katherine Kantor
Prepress technician: Katherine Kantor
Project manager: Santosh Vasudevan (Q2AMEDIA)
Art direction: Rahul Dhiman (Q2AMEDIA)
Cover design: Chhaya Sajwan (Q2AMEDIA)
Design: Tarang Saggar (Q2AMEDIA)
Photo research: Sakshi Saluja (Q2AMEDIA)

Photographs: P3: Corbis (bottom left), Istockphoto (bottom right); P4: Softblue/BigStockPhoto; P5: Mark Bond/Shutterstock, Istockphoto (bottom right); P6: Q2A Media Art Bank; P7: Pichugin Dmitry/ Shutterstock; P8: JTB Photo/Photolibrary; P9: Phil Emmerson/ Shutterstock (top), Istockphoto (bottom right); P10: David R Frazier/ Photolibrary; P11: Peter Steiner/Alamy (top right), Istockphoto (bottom right); P12: David Lyons/Alamy; P13: Lester Lefkowitz/ Photolibrary; P14: Martyn Unsworth/Istockphoto; P15: Mbl/Photolibrary; P16: Sue Anderson/Ecoscene (bottom), Istockphoto (bottom left); P17: S.Portland/Wikipedia; P18: Martin Bond/Photolibrary; P19: Chris Harvey/Shutterstock (top), V. J. Matthew/Shutterstock (bottom); P20: Peter Treanor/Alamy (bottom), Istockphoto (bottom right); P21: JanP/Shutterstock; P22: John Howard/SPL/ Photolibrary; P23: Zhen Yang/Istockphoto; P24: James L. Lauser/ Shutterstock; P25: The London Art Archive/Alamy; P26: Millan/ Dreamstime; P27: Kevin Schafer/Alamy; P28: Ng Han Guan/AP Images (bottom), Istockphoto (bottom right); P29: Greenshoots Communications/Alamy; P30: Dr Jeremy Burgess/SPL (top); P30: Liquid Light/Alamy (bottom); P31: Doug Baines/Shutterstock

Cover: www.soton.ac.uk

Title page: Matt Niebuhr/Shutterstock

Library and Archives Canada Cataloguing in Publication

Peppas, Lynn
    Ocean, tidal and wave energy : power from the sea / Lynn Peppas.

(Energy revolution)
Includes index.

ISBN 978-0-7787-2919-8 (bound).--ISBN 978-0-7787-2933-4 (pbk.)

    1. Ocean energy resources--Juvenile literature. I. Title. II. Series.

TC147.P46 2008   j333.91'4   C2008-901526-6

Library of Congress Cataloging-in-Publication Data

Peppas, Lynn.
    Ocean, tidal, and wave energy : power from the sea / Lynn Peppas.
        p. cm. -- (Energy revolution)
    Includes index.
    ISBN-13: 978-0-7787-2933-4 (pbk. : alk. paper)
    ISBN-10: 0-7787-2933-8 (pbk. : alk. paper)
    ISBN-13: 978-0-7787-2919-8 (reinforced library binding : alk. paper)
    ISBN-10: 0-7787-2919-2 (reinforced library binding : alk. paper)
    1. Tidal power--Juvenile literature. 2. Ocean energy resources--Juvenile literature. 3. Tidal power-plants--Juvenile literature. I. Title. II. Series.

TC147.P47 2008
621.31'2134--dc22
                                                2008019923

Crabtree Publishing Company

www.crabtreebooks.com   1-800-387-7650

Published in Canada
Crabtree Publishing
616 Welland Ave.
St. Catharines, ON
L2M 5V6

Published in the United States
Crabtree Publishing
PMB16A
350 Fifth Ave., Suite 3308
New York, NY 10118

Published in the United Kingdom
Crabtree Publishing
White Cross Mills
High Town, Lancaster
LA1 4XS

Published in Australia
Crabtree Publishing
386 Mt. Alexander Rd.
Ascot Vale (Melbourne)
VIC 3032

Contents

4   **Energy in Our Lives**

6   **Helping Our Planet**

8   **What Is Water?**

10   **The Power of Water**

12   **Storing Water**

14   **Geothermal Energy**

16   **Waves of the Future**

18   **Good Tidings**

20   **Running on Water**

22   **History of Water Power**

26   **The Drawbacks**

28   **Making the Change**

30   **Timeline**

32   **Glossary and Index**

Energy Conservation: "We Can Do It!"

"We Can Do It" was a slogan that appeared on posters made during **World War II**. One poster featured "Rosie the Riveter," a woman dressed in blue coveralls (shown below). The poster was originally intended to encourage women to enter the workforce in industry to replace the men who left to serve in the war. Today, the image of Rosie the Riveter represents a time when people came together as a society to reach a common goal. Today's energy challenge can be combated in a similar way. Together, we can work to save our planet from the pollution caused by burning **fossil fuels**. We can learn to conserve energy and develop alternative energy sources.

Energy in Our Lives

Energy is a part of our daily lives. Whenever we heat our homes, prepare our food, or drive in a car, we use energy. Energy makes things happen. Living things need energy to grow and survive. People, animals, and plants cannot live without it.

Hydroelectric power plants, like this one at the Hoover Dam in the United States, use water to power turbines that produce electricity. The electricity is moved through power lines to places that need it.

What Is Energy?

Scientists define energy as the **capacity**, or ability, to do work or make things happen. For example, water by itself cannot do work. It contains only **potential energy**, or the future ability to do work. If water were to flow over a cliff and fall toward the ground, the force of the falling water would produce **kinetic**, or moving, energy. The kinetic energy of the water can do work. It can turn a water wheel or **turbine** and produce another kind of energy, called electricity. The amount of energy produced is measured in joules. This is not the same as the rate at which energy is used, which is called power. Power is measured in watts or joules per second.

Forms of Energy

Energy cannot be created or destroyed but it can be transferred, or moved from one thing to another. When an animal eats a plant, the energy in the plant is transferred into the animal. Energy can also be converted, or changed, from one form to another. When **thermal**, or heat, energy is added to water, it changes from a liquid state to a gas and produces energy in the form of **steam**. This steam is used to power turbines that then generate electricity. The energy of the steam is then converted into electricity. Energy is converted into different forms, such as electricity, so that it can be moved easily from one location to another.

Energy Sources

Energy sources can be either non-renewable or renewable. Fossil fuels, such as coal, petroleum, and natural gas, are non-renewable sources of energy. Once they are used, they cannot be replaced. Renewable energy sources, such as water, the Sun, and **biomass** are continually replaced by nature or by people.

Waves in oceans contain energy. Their potential to do work must be collected by turbines and transformed by generators so the energy can be used by people.

Conservation Tip

Energy conservation means reducing the amount of power that we use. You can find tips on how to conserve energy and facts about energy conservation in boxes like these.

Helping Our Planet

Most of the energy people use to power factories or drive vehicles comes from fossil fuels, such as coal, oil, or natural gas. Fossil fuels release energy when they are burned, but they also pollute the environment. The Sun, wind, and water, are renewable energy sources. They do not pollute the environment.

Burning Fossil Fuels

All matter is made from particles called atoms and molecules that bond together. Energy keeps these particles together. Fossil fuels release their energy when a heat source is added to them. The particles that keep them together break up, and energy is released. This process is called chemical energy. When fossil fuels are burned for fuel, they release energy but they also release harmful emissions into our atmosphere. One of these harmful emissions is carbon dioxide.

When coal and oil are "burned" or used for energy, they mix with moisture in the air to create acid rain. Acid rain is a pollution that destroys lakes and the marine life in them.

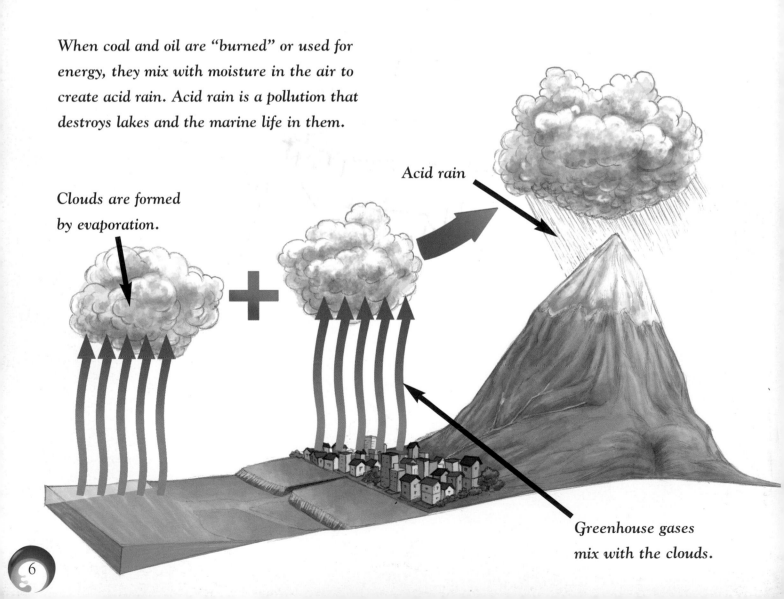

Clouds are formed by evaporation.

Acid rain

Greenhouse gases mix with the clouds.

Global Warming

Carbon dioxide is a greenhouse gas that traps Earth's heat in the atmosphere. Some greenhouse gases occur naturally and are important in keeping the planet at a comfortable temperature for people, plants, and animals. An increase in the use of fossil fuels for energy has increased the amount of carbon dioxide released into the atmosphere. This traps more heat than is needed. This increase in Earth's average temperatures is called **global warming**. Many scientists believe that rising temperatures will cause extreme weather conditions, such as droughts, **floods**, and storms.

Fossil fuels, such as coal, cause damage to the environment by releasing poisonous gases when they are burned.

What Is Water?

Water is a natural resource that covers about 70 percent of Earth's surface. People cannot live without water. We depend on it for many things, such as drinking, watering crops, washing, and as a source of energy. As the need to create new sources for energy grows, water becomes even more important in our lives.

H₂O

One molecule of water is made of two hydrogen atoms and one oxygen atom. This is why scientists call water H_2O. Atoms are the smallest particles that make up everyday objects. Molecules of water are so small they cannot be seen without high-powered microscopes used in science laboratories.

From Water to Energy

Everything on Earth is made up of matter. Water is a type of matter that has energy because of its ability to change states easily by adding, or taking away, energy. Water molecules are constantly moving. Every molecule of water contains the energy that keeps it together. Water exists in three states, or forms: as a solid in the form of ice, as a liquid that flows in oceans and lakes, or as steam, that you can see as a cloud rising from a boiling pot of water. When heat energy is taken away from liquid water and it is cooled to 32° Fahrenheit (0° Celsius), the molecules move very slowly, and change to ice. When heat energy is added to liquid water, the molecules move faster and farther apart and change to **water vapor**, or steam. When water changes from a liquid to a vapor, the energy created by this change can be harnessed, or gathered, to do work.

Flowing water in waterfalls contains a lot of energy that can be tapped for electric power generation.

The Water Cycle

Water is a renewable source of energy. Water is being constantly recycled through a natural process called the water cycle. **Solar energy,** or the energy of the Sun, gives heat energy to everything on Earth, and warms bodies of water. Heat energy that comes from the Sun powers the water cycle. It warms surface water, and causes the water to **evaporate**, or change from a liquid to a vapor. This warmer vapor rises into the atmosphere where it cools and changes back into water droplets that form clouds. The clouds move and release rain or snow that falls to the ground. Liquid water that falls on the ground runs back into streams, rivers, and oceans where it is **recycled** all over again.

Water is evaporating from lakes, rivers, and ponds to form water vapor, making the water cycle a continuous process.

Conservation Tip

Collect the water you use for rinsing clothes and utensils and reuse it to water your garden. This will help reduce pollution.

9

The Power of Water

For thousands of years, the power of water has been harnessed by using the rivers that flow into Earth's seas and oceans. Energy gathered from moving water is called hydroelectricity. Hydro is the Greek word for water. Electricity is a source of energy that can heat homes, turn on lights, and run computers. The energy of moving water must go through three steps before providing electricity to homes and businesses. The moving water is first used to turn turbines. Then a generator converts the energy from the turbine into electrical energy. Finally, a **power grid** carries the electricity over great distances so it can be used where it is needed.

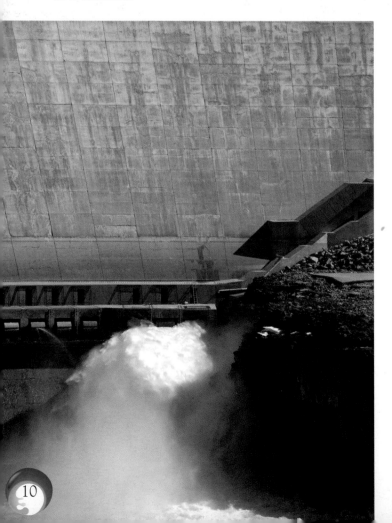

Run of the River

Hydroelectric power stations are built near fast-flowing rivers and often near waterfalls. Sometimes a **dam** is built across the river to contain the water. This creates a huge man-made lake called a **reservoir**. The water in the rivers and reservoirs can then be channeled through a penstock, or pipes that redirect the flow of water. Since the year 1896, the Niagara River has provided hydroelectric power to residents in the United States and Canada. Not all of the water is used for hydroelectric power, however.

The Turbine

The energy of fast-moving water comes from rushing through a turbine. A turbine is a large, round cylinder with a shaft in the center, and curved blades surrounding it. A turbine looks like a fan. From the center of this set of turbine blades rises a long pipe known as a shaft. The fans are enclosed by a metal body or chamber. The chamber has one inlet for water to flow in and an outlet through which water can flow out. Water moving at high speeds is fed into the container through the inlet. The speed of the moving water hits the blades of the turbine. As a result, the fan starts spinning at a very high speed. The spinning fan causes the shaft to rotate at an equally high speed. The moving water then flows out of the chamber.

Hydroelectric dams contain water and release it from great heights to power turbines.

The Generator

A generator is a device that changes the kinetic energy of the moving shaft of the turbine into electrical energy. A generator works with magnets and a coil of wire. The coil of wire is spun around by the turbine's shaft. The shaft itself is bracketed by two huge magnets. The coil of wire produces an electrical current when it rotates between the two stationary magnets that are located on either side of the shaft. The current produced by the generator is known as alternating current (AC). The current produced by generators is a low voltage current. Voltage is the measurement of the pressure under which electricity moves. This low voltage current is then gathered and sent through cables to a **transformer**. Electricity travels more efficiently at a high voltage. Thus, these transformers change the low voltage alternating current produced by the generators into a current of very high voltage for easy transmission through long distances.

The Power Grid

The final step is to **transport**, or move, the energy to where it is needed by a power-distribution grid called a power grid. This is done using cables called power lines. These power lines carry the high-voltage current to wherever electricity is needed. When the electrical energy reaches its destination, it must pass through another transformer that will change the high voltage current back into a low voltage current so that it can be used by factories, businesses, and homes.

In a hydroelectric power plant, the structure that houses the turbines and generators is called the powerhouse.

Conservation Tip

Turn the lights off when you are leaving a room. Saving electricity means saving the environment.

11

Storing Water

Hydroelectric energy plants need large amounts of moving water to produce electricity. To direct and store large amounts of water, people construct dams across rivers that stop the water's natural flow. The water that is held back is called a reservoir. Dams store water to be used for energy. The reservoirs they create also supply water for people, animals, and crops in dry areas where droughts occur. In very wet areas, dams help to control flooding.

Dams are built across rivers to create reservoirs. Water from the reservoir is channeled through pipes to the turbines to produce electricity. Excessive water is drained out of the dam with the help of spillways.

Dams

A dam is a barrier that blocks the flow of a waterway. In nature, beavers build dams made of mud, stones, and branches across small streams. Dams that people build are some of the largest, and most expensive, man-made structures in the world. People construct dams using earth, rock, steel, and concrete, depending on the design of the dam. Dams must be very strong to hold back so much water.

Reservoir and Turbines

Stored water is directed from the reservoir to the turbines of the hydroelectric plant through large, steel, sluice gates. The water travels through pipes called penstocks. Some dams have spillways that allow excess water to drain.

The Hoover Dam

The Hoover Dam on the Colorado River, between Nevada and Arizona, is a curved gravity dam that was built to store water to generate hydroelectric power. To build the 726-foot (221-meter) tall, concrete dam, thousands of workers had to redirect the Colorado River through four tunnels dug through the surrounding canyon walls.

Construction of the dam was finished in 1936, and at that time, it was the largest dam ever built. Today it is the 18th highest dam in the world. The Hoover Dam holds back over 1 trillion cubic feet (28 billion cubic meters) of water in its reservoir at Lake Mead.

The Hoover Dam on the Colorado River weighs more than 6,600,000 tons.

Waves of the Future

Ocean waves are powerful sources of energy. Over time, they can even wear away and break solid rock. The energy from moving waves in the ocean can be harnessed to produce electricity. Two types of energy generation devices, called floating and fixed devices, can be used to capture a wave's energy and change it into electricity. Electricity can be transferred from these devices to electrical power lines and travel to onshore locations where the energy is needed. The western coasts of Scotland, Canada, southern Africa, Australia, and the northwestern coasts of the United States are locations where wave power may be developed in the future.

Sun, Wind, and Waves

Wave power begins with the Sun. Solar energy creates the winds that blow across a large body of water, such as an ocean. The Sun heats the air, and the warm air rises. Cooler air rushes in to take the place of the warm air that has risen and creates wind. Waves are caused by the winds that blow over the water's surface.

The Islay Wave Power Station uses the power of waves to create enough electricity for around 500 homes on the island of Islay, off the coast of Scotland.

Conservation Tip

Take short showers instead of baths to save water and energy. Turn the water off when you are lathering up. Turn it back on to rinse off.

Floating Wave Energy

Floating wave energy devices rest on the water's surface, usually far from shore. There are different designs of floating wave energy devices. One of these devices is called the Salter Duck floating wave energy device. The motions of waves makes the Salter Duck move up and down. This movement swings a **pendulum** back and forth inside the device that turns a turbine. The turbine produces electricity.

Fixed Wave Energy

Fixed wave energy devices use the movement of waves to generate electricity. One of these is the Oscillating Water Column. Waves push air into a chamber in the machine. The air is forced up, turning a turbine. When the wave draws back, the air moves down the chamber, turning the turbine again. The stream of air moves a generator that changes energy into electricity.

CASE STUDY

Wave Farms

Scientists have just begun to explore energy generated from waves. The first commercial wave farm was opened in Portugal, in southwestern Europe, in 2006. The wave farm uses a long, floating device called the Pelamis P-750 that sits on top of the water, but is partly submerged. Each Pelamis P-750 wave energy converter is 459 feet (140 meters) long, and 11.5 feet (3.5 meters) in diameter. Three of these wave energy converters are located about 3 miles (4.8 kilometers) away from Portugal's northern Atlantic coast. Waves move the hinged sections of the Pelamis P-750, and energy from the movement powers a generator. The generator changes the energy into electricity. This electrical energy is transported to shore through a wire cable that runs along the bottom of the sea.

The Pelamis P-750 was developed by the Scottish company Pelamis Wave Power. It was the world's first machine to generate electricity from waves.

Good Tidings

Earth's oceans are constantly rising and falling in powerful tides. During high tide, water floods in toward shore. During low tide, water rushes away from shore. Tides occur everyday, and in most areas occur twice a day, so tidal movement supplies a steady source of energy. Scientists have discovered ways to harness the energy of an ocean's tidal movements by building a tidal barrage across the wide mouth of a river.

What is Tidal Power?

Tidal power, or tidal energy, converts the energy of tides into electricity. Tides are caused by the effects of gravity created by Earth's rotation and the pull of the Sun and Earth's Moon. The stronger the tide in speed or height, the more energy is produced. Tidal energy is not yet widely used, but researchers are working on new tidal energy technology. There are two types of tidal power: tidal stream power and barrages.

In 1967, the world's first tidal power station, the La Rance tidal power station, was built in northern France. The turbines in the station gather enough energy to give power to 250,000 homes.

Ocean Energy

Tides move Earth's oceans all the time, and moving water has energy. The energy from tides can be collected and converted by tidal barrages that are built across an **estuary**, or wide mouth of a river where fresh water meets the salt water of an ocean. When rain and other precipitation falls on land, it is either absorbed or becomes runoff that flows downhill into rivers and lakes, making its way back to an ocean. An estuary is the point where the river's freshwater meets the saltwater from the ocean, as it rises or falls in tides. A tidal barrage stretches across an estuary from one point of land to another. It can also be used as a bridge for vehicles to travel on.

The turbines on a tidal barrage turn as water moves across them into the mouth of the river and back out, powering generators.

Tidal Barrages at Work

A tidal barrage works much like a dam because it harnesses the power of moving water through turbines and generators, but instead of gathering energy from falling water, it gathers the energy of the tides as they move into the river and then back out again. The flow of water from an incoming tide moves bulb-shaped turbines underwater. Sluice gates, made from aluminum and steel, and located on both sides of the tidal barrage are opened when the tide comes in, and then closed. As the tide goes out, water levels drop, and sluice gates are opened, allowing the water to rush out. This rushing water powers bulb turbines, which then power generators to convert the energy into electricity.

The Bay of Fundy between Nova Scotia and New Brunswick, Canada, has some of the highest tides in the world. The Annapolis Royal Generating station is one of only three tidal barrage generating stations in the world.

Running on Water

Many people believe that water holds the key to solving the world's future energy needs. Scientists, governments, and private companies in many countries are exploring ways to use hydrogen, an odorless, colorless gas that is found in water, to generate affordable power without polluting the environment. Recent research has led to the development of the hydrogen fuel cell, that combines hydrogen and oxygen chemically to produce electricity, water, and waste heat.

Normal internal combustion engines emit a lot of harmful gases such as carbon monoxide resulting in large scale pollution.

What Is Hydrogen?

Hydrogen is found throughout the universe. On Earth, hydrogen is almost always found as part of other substances, such as plants and animals, fossil fuels, and water. When hydrogen is removed from these substances, it can be used to carry energy to fuel cells, which can generate electricity. Fuel cells can be used to power vehicles, such as cars, trucks, and buses, as well as homes, office buildings, and factories. Some countries are working toward using hydrogen fuel cells instead of fossil fuels for heat and power. Switching to hydrogen made from clean, renewable energy sources will take a long time and cost a lot of money to complete.

Conservation Tip

Too many vehicles on roads emit harmful gases. Talk to your neighbors and check out options for carpooling to school or work to conserve energy.

Water Splitting

One way to create hydrogen from a renewable source is to use water. Water is made up of tiny particles of matter called atoms. Two atoms of hydrogen bond, or join, with one atom of oxygen to make each molecule of water. In order to generate energy, the atoms of oxygen and hydrogen have to be separated from each other, freeing the hydrogen. The most common way to separate hydrogen from water is by running an electrical current through the water. Electricity breaks the bond that holds the hydrogen and oxygen atoms together. This process is called electrolysis. If the electric current is generated using renewable energy sources, such as wind, solar, geothermal, or hydroelectric power, there will be no harmful gas emissions from electrolysis. The hydrogen gas can then be stored and delivered to places that will turn it into energy.

Fuel Cells and the Future

Hydrogen can be turned into usable energy through fuel cells. Fuel cells are devices that create electricity by combining hydrogen and oxygen. One fuel cell can generate enough power for devices such as cell phones or digital cameras. Fuel cells can also be stacked together to generate even more electricity. Fuel cell stacks can be used to power cars, trucks, ships, and even submarines. NASA has been using fuel cell stacks on space missions for many years. Large fuel cell stacks can generate enough power for homes or buildings. In the future, they may power entire towns. Fuel cells generate electricity without any harmful emissions. Water is the only emission a fuel cell makes. The water can then be recycled to produce hydrogen through electrolysis. This perfect cycle of water to hydrogen and back to water again could form the foundation of a hydrogen economy for the future.

Hydrogen-powered fuel cells hold enormous promise as a power source for a future generation of cars.

History of Water Power

People have been using moving water as a source of energy for thousands of years. Societies built their mills at the source of moving water, or redirected that source of water through a canal or **aqueduct** to come to a mill. Mills were used to grind wheat or grain into flour. Water wheels were used by ancient peoples to help do work but needed to be located at a fast moving source of water such as a river or a stream. The problem was that not everyone had access to large, moving sources of water. Historically, people could not convert the energy from moving water and deliver it to wherever it was needed, as we can today.

Water Wheels

The water wheel is an ancient invention used by people from China, the Middle East, and Rome. The first modern vertical water wheel was invented by Roman architect Vitruvius in A.D. 27. Water wheels use the energy from moving water to turn paddles or curved blades to do work. They resemble modern turbines. There are three types of water wheels: a horizontal water wheel, and two types of vertical water wheels, the undershot wheel, and the overshot wheel.

The water flowing in the river would turn wheels that were connected to gears.

A Flour Mill

The Flour Mill at Barbegal, France was built in A.D. 300, and was one of the largest known water wheel systems. Water traveled through an aqueduct to the top of the mill site where it was directed through 16 large vertical water wheels, located from the top to the bottom of a hillside. There were two rows of eight water wheels. The water would generate energy through one wheel and then fall into the next underneath it, traveling downhill through each of the eight mills. The grain made from the Berbegal mill was said to have fed 12,500 people living in Arles, France.

Mills use water power to grind coarse grains into flour.

Horizontal Water Wheels

The horizontal water wheel has paddles on the bottom of a center shaft, that turned a rotor, or millstone, on top. Water was directed to turn the paddles, which turned the shaft and rotor. These types of water wheels were used in Europe and China in 2000 B.C. to turn a millstone to grind grains.

Vertical Water Wheels

Vertical wheels can harness and generate more power than horizontal water wheels. They have a horizontal axis on which a large wheel with paddles turns to do work. The undershot wheel is turned by the flow of water underneath the wheel, usually from a shallow stream or river with a strong current. This water wheel rotates a shaft that turns gears to convert the energy of moving water to move the millstones for grinding grain. Overshot wheels are the most efficient and powerful wheels of them all, but water must be poured from the top of the wheel to harness the moving water's energy. During ancient times, people had to build special canals and channels to bring the water needed to move these giant wheels.

Steam Power

Ancient peoples who did not live near a river discovered another way to gather energy from water. Water has energy when heat energy is added to it, and it evaporates, from a liquid to a vapor. Early scientists used energy of steam to work engines that would later power factories and trains.

Hero of Alexandria

In A.D. 62, a Greek inventor, Hero of Alexandria, invented the first steam engine, called an "aeolipile." The aeolipile harnessed the energy from water changing states from a liquid to steam. Hero's steam engine was a hollow ball that had two exhaust pipes on opposite sides. Underneath the hollow ball was a fire pit.

Hero filled the ball with water, and placed it over the fire. When the water began to boil and produced steam, the steam escaped from the pipes and made the ball spin. Hero's steam engine did not do any work for him, but it did prove that when water changed states from a liquid to steam, its energy could be harnessed to do the work to make the ball spin.

Boyle's Law

In 1660, a British scientist named Robert Boyle created a series of laws that explained how gases behave at different temperatures and pressures. Boyle's Law explained that vapor molecules such within a contained space exerted a certain amount of pressure as they moved and collided, or bounced against, their container. When heat was taken away from the container, the molecules moved slower, collided less, and exerted less pressure. When heat was added to the container, the molecules moved and collided even more, and created a greater pressure within the container. Boyle's Law states that when more heat energy is added to steam, it gains energy to do more work.

Steam engines powered steam locomotives.

The Piston Steam Engine

Other scientists used Boyle's Law to invent their own steam-powered engines. A French scientist named Denis Papin invented the first piston steam engine in 1690. Papin's invention showed that the **pressure**, or energy, of steam could do the work of pushing a piston. A piston is a sliding shaft within a fitted cylinder. A British scientist, Thomas Savery, built the first working steam engine in 1698, that was later improved upon by an English blacksmith named Thomas Newcomen, in 1705, and by a Scottish inventor, James Watt, in 1776. In 1799, English inventor, Richard Trevithick, began using steam engines that powered vehicles called steam locomotives. In 1802, he built the first steam railway locomotive that carried large loads of iron over great distances.

Industrial Revolution

The new inventions of steam engines that could harness the energy from steam helped power the **Industrial Revolution**. For the first time, factories all around the world could **mass produce**, or produce in large quantities, their merchandise. Steam engines became a reliable source of energy. Factories could be located anywhere, not just along moving rivers or streams. Steam locomotives could transport the goods produced by factories and textile mills.

Steam Power

A steam engine works when heat energy is added to water. When water is heated, it evaporates, and turns into vapor, or steam. The heated steam molecules spread apart and bounce off each other and the walls of the container at a faster rate. This exerts a pressure against a piston. This pressure pushes the piston up a fitted cylinder. The movement of the piston pushes a connecting rod, which turns a flywheel. When the steam is allowed to expand, its heat energy is used up, and it cools, producing less pressure, and another connecting rod pushes the piston back in place so that steam can push it up again. The piston uses the heat energy from the steam and changes it into mechanical energy of the piston's movement.

A steam engine works when heat energy is added to water.

The Drawbacks

People have been putting water's energy to work for them for many years. Still, there are some drawbacks to using water as an energy source. The large human-made structures, such as dams and tidal barrages, that are needed to harness water's energy can destroy natural habitats by altering the course of rivers and coasts. Violent ocean storms can destroy tidal turbines or smash wave farms. In addition, the cost of building the technologies to harness water's power are also high.

Environmental Effects

Since so much of the world depends on water, any disruption to its natural flow will have damaging effects on the environment. When dams are built to block the natural flow of water from rivers, reservoirs and lakes are created that flood areas where animals and plants once existed. This flooding destroys entire **ecosystems**. Rivers also carry very small soil and rock particles called silt that acts as a fertilizer for flat lands beside rivers known as flood plains. If the silt cannot get to the flood plains, the soil in the flood plains does not receive important nutrients and may be destroyed.

Dam construction destroys natural environments and changes the way rivers flow.

Weather Conditions

Wave farms depend on specific weather conditions. They need surface ocean waves that provide a steady source of movement in the water and allows wave generation devices to convert energy. On moderately windy days, these generation devices lie on top of the water and transfer energy to create electricity that is shipped onshore. Weather conditions are always changing, making waves an unreliable energy source. On calm days with very little wind, there are no waves to generate power. Severe storms with high winds create giant waves that can damage the expensive wave generation devices.

The Cost of Water Power

Dams are the most expensive and largest structures made by people. Although dams are built for many uses, such as storing water for use in dry seasons, hydroelectric power stations often depend on them to store water for energy purposes. These can cost millions of dollars to build.

Fish ladders such as the one in this image allow fish to cross artificial barriers created across rivers. This is but one step taken so that the construction of dams and barrages does not disrupt the ecosystem in the river and fish continue to follow the same patterns that they are used to.

The Perks

Dams, barrages, wave generation power stations, and geothermal power plants cost millions of dollars to build. To save money, some power stations can even pump the water already used to convert energy back up to the reservoir. This way, the same water is used again and again. Water energy also does not release harmful pollutants into the air the way that fossil fuel powered plants do.

Making the Change

Burning fossil fuels harms the environment. We need cleaner, renewable sources of energy such as water to generate power for heating homes, operating factories, and driving vehicles. Making the change from fossil fuels to alternative energy sources such as water for energy is already underway, but to keep up with the growing demands for energy, more power stations that convert the energy in water will be needed. These changes will take time, money, and planning.

Hydroelectric power plants supply clean sources of electricity.

Demand and Supply

The demand for more "clean" energy sources is growing. About one third of the world's population does not use electrical energy, but as the **standard of living** improves and populations grow, the need for cleaner sources of energy will also grow. Hydroelectric power plants supply clean sources of electricity worldwide, and produce about three percent of the world's energy needs. More power plants are needed to keep up with demand. Many ideal sites are already being used to generate hydroelectricity so scientists are exploring new ways to tap into the power of water.

Conservation Tip

A leaky faucet can waste gallons of water. If your faucet leaks, let your parents know so it can be fixed. Make sure you turn your faucet off completely each time you use it.

Three Gorges Dam

The Three Gorges Dam in China is still under construction. When it is finished in 2009, it will be the largest hydroelectric dam in the world. It will generate twice the power of the Itaipu Dam in Brazil. The Three Gorges Dam will be 1.5 miles (2.4 kilometers) wide, and more than 597 feet (182 meters) high and will create a reservoir that is almost 400 miles (643 kilometers) long. More than 250,000 workers have been building it for over 15 years. The hydroelectric power station will provide a cleaner source of power for China's factories and industries. The dam was also built to prevent flooding in nearby areas. The huge reservoir will allow ships to transport goods inland.

Ideas for the Future

Today, scientists are turning to the power of the oceans for new sources of energy. Scientists are working on an Ocean Thermal Energy Conversion to tap the energy of changing water temperatures in the ocean. Water at the surface of the ocean near the equator has an average temperature of 77° Fahrenheit (25° Celsius). The Ocean Thermal Energy Device uses a liquid that evaporates at a low temperature of 78° Fahrenheit (27° Celsius). The vapor from the liquid drives a turbine attached to a generator that changes energy into electricity. Water from the ocean's bottom cools the vapor so that it condenses back to a liquid to be used again to generate electricity.

Modern ocean-based structures harness the power of ocean currents to generate clean electricity.

Timeline

Hero of Alexandria created the world's first steam engine.

The water wheel is one of the oldest sources of power.

Water has played an important role in human history. Thousands of years ago, people discovered the energy produced from water could power machines that help them work. Today, this energy has become even more important. Many who have depended on fossil fuels for energy are turning to alternative sources of energy and new energy producing technologies to harness the power of water.

8000 B.C

People use hot springs (geothermal energy or heated water from the earth) for bathing and heating.

2000 B.C.

Ancient writers from China and the Middle East describe early water wheels and how they help to do work such as grinding grains.

A.D. 27

Roman architect Vitruvius invents the modern water wheel.

A.D. 62

Greek inventor Hero invents the first steam engine, called the "aeolipile."

1698

British scientist Thomas Savery builds the first working steam engine.

1705

Savery's model was improved upon by Thomas Newcomen, and later by James Watt, in 1776.

1776

British scientist, Henry Cavendish discovers hydrogen.

1800

William Nicholson and Anthony Carlisle discover that water can be split into hydrogen and oxygen using electrolysis.

1820

Michael Faraday, builds the first electricity generator.

1838

German scientist Christian Schonbein has the idea that combining hydrogen and oxygen could create an electric current and water. This led to the invention of the first fuel cell.

1880

American inventor, Lester Allan Pelton, invents the water turbine.

1882

The first hydroelectric power plant is built in Appleton, Wisconsin.

1884

British engineer, Sir Charles Parsons invents the steam turbine that gathers the energy from steam.

1904

Energy from steam is produced in Larderello Fields in Italy for the first time.

1966

La Rance, in France is the first commercial tidal power plant

1974

Stephen Salter invents the Salter Duck, a floating wave generation device.

Steam is the most widely used source of energy derived from water.

Glossary

aqueduct An artificial channel for conveying water

biomass The total amount of all living things within a specific volume or environment

carbon monoxide A toxic gas produced by burning of various fuels

combustion Chemical oxidation that generates light and heat

dam A man-made structure constructed on a river to control the flow of water

commercial Dealing with business or trade, the activity of buying and selling

ecosystem A complete community of living organisms and the nonliving materials of their surroundings

estuary A semi-enclosed body of water with one or more rivers and streams flowing into it

flood The rising of a body of water and its overflowing onto normally dry land

fossil fuels Fuels such as coal, oil, natural gas, etc. that result from the compression of ancient plant and animal life formed over millions of years

generator A device that converts mechanical energy into electrical energy

global warming An increase in the surface temperature of Earth. Caused by emissions of greenhouse gases

gravity The force that pulls one object toward another

hot spring A natural spring producing warm water

Industrial Revolution A period starting in the late 1700s in England, when people began moving to cities to work in factories

pendulum A weight hung from a fixed point so that it can swing freely backward and forward

power plant A facility where power, especially electricity, is generated

power grid Distributes electricity throughout an area using high tension cables

recycle Reprocessing of old matter or substance

reservoir A huge man-made lake built on a river

standard of living The degree of wealth and comfort available to a person or community

steam Water in vapor form, which is used as the working fluid in steam turbines

transformer A device that converts the generator's low-voltage electricity to higher-voltage levels for transmission to a city or factory

turbine A device in which mechanical power is created by making steam, air, or flowing water

World War II A war (1939–45) between the Axis Powers (Germany, Italy, and Japan) and the Allies (United Kingdom, the Soviet Union, and the United States)

Index

acid rain 6
case study 13, 15, 17, 23, 29
dams 4, 10, 12-13, 19, 26, 27, 29
ecosystem 26, 27
emission 6, 21
fish ladder 27
fossil fuels 5-7, 20, 27, 28, 30

generators 5, 10, 11, 14, 17, 19, 29, 31
geothermal energy 14-15, 27, 30
geyser 14
gravity 13, 18
hydroelectricity 10, 12, 13, 21, 27, 28, 29, 31
hydrogen 8, 20, 21, 31

Industrial Revolution 25
kinetic energy 4, 11
NASA 21
Niagara River 10
pollution 6, 9, 20
power grid 10-11
reservoir 10, 12, 13, 15, 26, 27, 29
Salter Duck 17, 31

sluice gate 12, 19
steam 4, 8, 14, 24-25, 30, 31
tidal barrage 18, 19, 26, 27
tidal power 18-19, 31
turbines 4, 5, 10, 11, 12, 14, 17, 19, 22, 26, 29, 31
water cycle 9
waves 5, 16-17, 26, 27, 31
water wheels 22-23, 30

Printed in the U.S.A.